Lunette

Pamela Davis

ABZ Series in Poetry

For Don,
My brother Jack Dillday thought
you might enjoy these poems
of love, life, loss, and art.
All good wishes with your book!
Pam

Lunette

poems by
Pamela Davis

ABZ

ABZ POETRY PRESS

All inquiries and permission requests should be addressed to the Editor,
ABZ Press, PO Box 2746, Huntington WV 25727-2746.

Cover by Myopia Design

CATALOGING DATA
Davis. Pamela
  Lunette / Pamela Davis.   1st ed.
  p.   cm. (ABZ First Book Poetry Series)
ISBN-13: 978-0-9801560-7-2 (pbk.   alk. paper)
ISBN-10: 0-9801560-7-2 (pbk.   alk. paper)

Library of Congress Control Number: 2014952844

I. Title. II. Series

CONTENTS

FOREWORD

A reader of Pamela Davis's *Lunette* cannot escape for a single page, or even a single line her amazing liveliness of language—it's alert to the world, deft with the word that will catch that world whirling past. Catch it and fix it—pinned to the page with a sardonic wit. Her speaker in the tour de force "The Female Line" is undeluded about the prospects for what women can do to derail the homicidal grand plans and glory that men are committed to:

> Indoors the men plan grand campaigns.
>
> We climb our yellow hair to the nursery, snatch baby boys
> From the fists of glory. *Go softly*—
>
> Forefathers watch from gilt frames. Uncles decant brandy,
> Straighten gold-braided shoulders. Downstairs, uniforms lie
>
> In wait for sons to fill them.

It's not just a liveliness of rhythm and wit, but also of wide-ranging reference. Baudelaire, and various painters, and Tippi Hedren out of Hitchcock's *The Birds*—they all make appearances, not to dazzle us with the breadth of …. Experience, but to signal the multiple ways she has of gaining depth. She marries an energy of language to a superb sense of story. And it's an energy of desire that the language mirrors perfectly—a desire to cherish what's fleeting and to rescue it from oblivion so it might furnish the soul with what the critic Kenneth Burke once called "equipment for living."

"I Want" is the title of a poem that begins:

> everything. Girlhood
> before first blood, my green Schwinn bike, barrettes, Dad's scotch-lit eyes.
> I want him back, and Uncle Dick dead at 32. Uncle Bob, 47.

Our poet is tough, but willing in "I Want" to trade:

> I give back the nights I drank straight through. The knife
> in my pocket. White vinyl boots.
> Lovers ran off, dogs.

It is a world that would be brutal if it were not so lucid—redeeming its extremity with a sense of urgent quest. "Hand to Hand" begins in a realm of violence and combat:

> My mother would raise one fist, fold her fury in, bitter
> Egg stirred to sour batter. Once for mocking her, she shut
> My mouth with the fry pan of her palm. I laughed, ran off,
>
> The slap stored as ember. Older, fighting with a lover, my own
> Hand rose quick as freak wind, flew to the side of his head.
> Shattered an ear drum. Fingers numb, I packed my things.

but discovers "another kind of man" just as tough as herself, present there to protect her. Passion and wit transform that crucial preposition and the "hand to hand" of combat becomes the two of them, gutsy equals who can progress "hand in hand, all heat and swagger."

Her poems accumulate a density of objects and an intensity of momentum—a rare combination. Things do not clutter her poem, they join the roll and tumble of the story force as if the poem were a mountain stream able to carry along anything smaller than a boulder—as in "Flight" :

> Above the coastal plain, low clouds thin to Spanish lace. Undo
>   Your shoulder blades, become the sleek wings
>   Of a mourning dove. Roll the bone bundles loose
> In their sockets. Where spine pinches nerve, gravity's straight pins bind.
>   Slip free. In this world, you have traveled as a stranger in heavy
>   Shoes. Unlace the leather, lift one bare foot. Then the other

These are bold poems—their tenderness is hidden in plain sight, their fierce brashness on prominent display and a spiritual yearning threatening to burst through every line. Read them and be enlivened.

Gregory Orr

For Chris

Lunette

1. A little moon, a satellite;
9. In the guillotine, the circular hole which receives the neck of the victim -- OED.

The Female Line

Squat, wrestle food from the furrow. Dash rags
on rock. Talk sass. Indoors the men plan grand campaigns.

We climb our yellow hair to the nursery, snatch baby boys
from the fists of glory. *Go softly*—

forefathers watch from gilt frames. Uncles decant brandy,
straighten gold-braided shoulders. Downstairs, uniforms lie

in wait for sons to fill them. The Brass pace corridors, wrists clasped
behind (their coats have marched ahead). Mother says

the teens need new sleeves. We take up the wool of our bodies
and knit them again. She means

the moon in us holds cemeteries and generals.

Bone Boy

Toddler from 400 AD, I find you at rest
under glass in an obscure room of a small
Paris museum. Little one, what bombs

thundered as you slept? What queens danced
in finery? Only a mother would take care
to set your body forever straight, your lips still

sweet with her milk. She spread your fingers—
pale as stripped twigs—into delicate fans. Once
they played over her face. How long before the sheer

casing of your skin let go? For the tendons that bound
you to shatter? Your spine intact, thin spindle
and half a skull. On your shoulder—sad epaulet—

your fallen jaw. I want to scoop you
up in my hands, tiptoe past museum guards,
borders. I'll make an altar of the things you missed—

skateboard, soccer ball. A final home for us
in the ruins of my womb.

Pourquoi Une Vache Rose?

The art teacher asks, pointing at Chagall's pink cow on a roof—
two little ones (babies? wolves?) at the teat—

      "Strawberry milk?"
                  (a few smirks)

Mademoiselle frowns, marches students on, red top knot
bobbing through galleries, white halls

      jugglers   bulls

           naked blue ladies
                (dawdlers dawdle)

Click click shoes rushing the boys
Dépêchez-vous—

      brides in the sky   skulls on the ground

          running man's round mouth
             (ohohohohoh)

Écoutez mes enfants!

      There will be gorgons   harlequins
         two-headed women—

Mortician's Daughter

I watch Dad slice the dinner roast with the same care
he uses to straighten a dead man's tie. Mortuary School taught anatomy, embalming.
Hair. For everything else, there's Fleshtone #3. In a suit and white shirt, he's like any dad

dropping his kids at school before work. He pulls away in a silver-finned limo, humming
The worms crawl in, the worms crawl out, the worms play
pinochle on your snout. One little worm is very shy, he crawls
in your ear and crawls out your eye.

After school I climb in and out of caskets
lined up like shiny cars—walnut and bronze in front, pine and metal in back.
Catching me, he flips the switch on/off on/off. I beg for light.

Ten, sneaky, I open the door to a Slumber Room, find a girl my age tucked
in a flocked coffin. Glossy doll lips. Tight blond curls. I reach to touch. Dad pulls
me back. His hands smell like biology frogs. *Don't worry*, he says,
Nobody you know is going to die.

*

My mother buys a black dress—my first—and gloves to stand at Dad's head. His box
is top of the line. Cream-tufted mahogany, lid half up. Half a man showing.

Under the velvet, he's barefoot. His watch and Masonic ring removed for oldest boy.

Alf in the back did the prep. Recast as granite, Dad's face is empty as a room stripped
of furniture. On his chest, his long, spider-haired hands are folded one on top

of the other as if he could reach up to adjust his own collar. I lean in,
smooth his lapel just so.

Blind Date with Baudelaire

He gallops to a stop in a silk-plumed carriage, cravat loose
at throat. I'm a party dress craving ruin. We careen mad
crooked streets. Down to the Seine. Up Montmartre's
butte. Charles unbuttons my skin to sniff my bones.
Summoning our future by moony lamplight,
his absinthe whisper, *we'll twine side by*
side. Pilgrims will come, read odes to
our stones. Leave roses. Red
granite kisses.

The night we wed, Charles
gives me his spleen.
Pourquoi pas? Two
poets—one dead,
one buried alive—
in the same
plot.

Birthdays

August night. Pirate sky. Brothers' big eyes on my cake twinking
sixteen, flesh pink frosting. Poof go the candles.
Daddy goes out.

The Summer of Love, I'm lost in jick jack fog. Stumble
up Union, flop on the floor. Up come fish hooks, an egg. Who's that
tip-toeing away?

In Paris, they say *Salut! Bon Anniversaire!* Fingers feed oysters,
mussels. *Sole meunière.* Birthday wishes on pale blue paper—

> *You're still our cake, baked*
> *in tinplate. Served on a sea star.*
> *P.S.* (Mom writes) *Come home quick, we're*
> *under new management—taking on water.*

New Daddy Blowfish drools. Smacks his gills on my silver scales,
little brown shoes next to Mother's heels. She signs over the house, flashes
a bossy new stone. He pats my thigh, *Let's have a toast.*
I take two.

Age 38, tiare flowers in my hair, I've come for birthday jewels—Tahitian pearls.
A lagoon. Jade-eyed man slips into my sleep, buttery rum mouth. He makes room
for me on the raft of his back, fine-sanded to satin, casts away.

Pony Ride

Asleep in my bed, I never heard the trucks roll in, spill men who never slept
into the hot August night. By noon, long, articulated arms

of carnival rides clawed flat sky, sent me spinning, sweet fried dough rising
in my throat. Fifteen, hungry for thrills

assembled on steel bolts, cages trembling on rusted-out joints. Tossed up,
slammed hard, the Hammer churned me like wash. Stopped

at the top, my cry soared over the crowd. *More! More!*

It's August again. Carnies are back setting up for the month. Veins like snakes,
one slow-steps a Shetland pony backward from a van. What became of the little mare

I rode at five—brown patches on white—rope-tethered to five others?
Heads slung low, they trudged a dung-rotted rut. Circling. Circling.

Dear Doris Day

I trusted you to never change
when I was 15 and wanted to believe men and women sat up talking all night

like the movie with you and Rock Hudson joking in bed, both in satin
pajamas buttoned to the chin. You were all that stood between my tyrant

hand and what waited for it under the sheet.

I believed you'd stay Rock's chum, immune
to Cary Grant's mink-lined smile. I'd be like you, beehive my hair, knees glued tight.

We'd drive forever, you, me and Rock in a two-tone Caddy he steered with a big, clean hand.

Instead you fell for a man with a moustache
filming *Teacher's Pet*. Simple plot—night school, Gable your student, you in twinset
and pearls, eyes growing big as pies

when he cocked one leg over the edge of your desk. I needed you
to report him to the authorities, not follow him to a nightclub. Later there'd be torn sheets,

cigarettes. Counting between periods.
Bad men with keys. But I never thought you'd go out of style, look back at me
from check stand tabloids.

You rescue stray dogs, the article said, and live alone.

I Want

everything. Girlhood
before first blood, my green Scwhinn bike, barrettes, Dad's scotch-lit eyes.
I want him back, and Uncle Dick dead at 32. Uncle Bob, 47.

The grandfather no one knew.

My brother's picture
tucked next to his body in the coffin. I want it to be the Halloween night he dressed
as an organ grinder, our little brother his monkey in a red felt vest.

I want 1961 again, watching JFK and Jackie fly
into the White House on magnificent hair. Before the Philco
took us to Dallas. Showed us Bobby in LA. Then Martin. In threes. Like us.

I give back the nights I drank straight through. The knife hidden
in my pocket. White vinyl boots.

Lovers ran off, dogs.

Now I hold tight.
At the sink my husband comes to me, belly friendly as a park bench. He backs my hip
against the tiles. In the mirror, steam collects like thieving mist from the past.

I clutch his waist, dig my fingers in.

The Wallow Variations

Before the stock market crashes for good,
and we're left defending our hour of pride, permit
me to digress—to wallow, so to speak, in excess.

Fill your pinched cheeks with warm air like a tuba
slowly blowing—*Wall-ow.*

Throw out your stocks, your bonds. Grow your portfolio
on the weightless wings of mission swallows. Pick up a horn,
follow fools. Yodel. Adopt a jobless broker.

Only ascetics eat aspic when marshmallows abound.
Better to dine on melons, Mallomars. Hot syrup waffles.
Look at the pigs wallowing in mud.
Do you still think them awful?

Imagine wrapping yourself in whatever you love—
Viennese waltzes, Whitman, Van Gogh.
(Behold the beautiful walleyed girl,
how her Picasso eyes wander all directions.)

There's no end to it, once you wade in. Your body
is wired for the perfect expression of yellow—
sunflowers, jonquils, full moonlight, champagne.
Wear them. Worship them. Ride over them in a barrel.

A wanton kiss is your Buddha blossoming.
Oh, my worried friend, take my word.

Elegy for Dead Words

Marie Smith Jones said good-bye to no one, there being no one alive
who knew the Eyak word for leave-taking.

She died in her sleep in the first month of a cold, young year. With her went
a place, and the history of a place, as happens when languages disappear,

as they do, twice again each moon. Crushed by army boot, absorbed
by redrawn borders, there are no words for what's gone missing—

Gods and songs and ways of cooking fish. In Queensland, a tribe who did not say *left*
or *right*, beheld one another as points on a compass. Believing trees and birds

were bound, the Eyak to the north, used a single sound
for leaf and feather. Mourn the lost consonants, the cloistered vowels.

Mourn Marie Smith Jones, the last of her tribe to put breath to word, word to wind.
Weep for Wappo, Barbareno, Akkala Sami, Ubykh—the echoes floating

from eastern Russia, the fallen sighs of the Southern Hemisphere.

Big Boy

The pigeons are at the feeder again, spilling husks,
nuts. Millet tumbles to the deck. Barefoot, I fly
at one clinging to the mesh like King Kong.

Get outta here Big Boy!

He flaps to the roof with other pot-bellied freeloaders
grandstanding just out of reach, his head thrust
like a drum major.

Eyeing me, he waits as I set out special seed
for songbirds who sing—so briefly—
before flying south.
.

Big Boy and I lurch through winter cold sober, moldy

coats drenched. Stumble-bumming for spoiled corn, he drops
half dollars of raw flop my dogs
mistake for yolks.

My bird book says pigeons can tell Picasso from a Monet.

What does Big Boy make of me—out at dawn, shaking
a stick—shouting as he lifts on slow wing,
now pearl, now zinc.

Childless

   I admit I'm afraid
of babies. They're damp, bad-eyed. Spontaneously enraged.
Someone's newborn gets handed over, a lump thrust into the nest of my arm. Wobble-headed,
it stares up. Glazed look of a newborn bat. It turns red. Howls, fist gripping my finger.

   Me, old fraud
kissing and cooing. More likely to sneak off with a lock of baby's gold
hair. The time one fell asleep on my chest—I remember this clearly—
a slight flutter in her opaline lid. I slowed my breath to rise and fall with hers.

   I never—
hardly ever—think of the other, unknown one, pulled from my womb.

   Close attachments,
sure. I've had dogs all my life. Sweet, obedient dogs I give children's names—
Sam, Fanny, Lou Lou.

   Shopping for a baby
shower, a mother watches me run my fingers over tiny buttons. Lift a onesie
to my cheek. While she hunts for change, I offer to hold her bundled child.

   The mother is wrong
to trust me. Half a chance I would bind the infant to my hip
until she took root. Shackle her ankles if she tried to walk.

   I touch the baby's coin
purse lips. When the mother pulls her child away,
my arms fall apart.

Hand to Hand

My mother would raise one fist, fold her fury in, bitter egg
added to sour batter. Once for mocking her, she shut
my mouth with the fry pan of her palm. I laughed, ran off,

the slap stored as ember. Older, fighting with a lover, my own
hand rose quick as freak wind, flew to the side of his head.
Shattered an eardrum. Fingers numb, I packed my things.

Twelve years later, I found another kind of man, wound my arms
around the warm rock of marriage. One summer day on State Street
he chased a boy for stealing my purse. Crushing the kid's wrist

in his grip, my husband forced him to his knees. *My hero*,
I cried. The boy crouched on the ground. Snot
and tears. On we walked, hand in hand, all heat and swagger.

Build to Suit

Seven trees leveled so far, the tree cutter braces his legs, chainsaw shaking
the length of him. Its shriek is the sound of rending—mutiny,
divorce. Muscle torn from bone.

The blade bullies into the heart of a rare Monterey Pine, limbs reaching
for the sky. Another branch shears off with a rush
of woody breath. Resin rises, meets the gash.

What's wrong with the trees? I shout over the roar.

The cutter stops the saw. Yanks at his headset. *Are they sick, the trees?*
He shrugs, returns to work. The pine drops like a man
shot in the back.

Night Mare

The wife is wild as an Indian pony. Withers bristling, she circles
the walls. A plank snags her mane. Backed against the gate,
her hooves paw straw. Hit stone.

She bows her head. Extends her lip to the moon in her pail.

A barren mare, bought on the cheap. It took rough hands, a crop to break
her. Still she shies the bit's cold clamp on her tongue. All night she frets.
He offers sticky oats. An apple. Nothing calms her.

To mount, he blindfolds her eyes, heaves a thick leg over her back.
Reins slice across her neck. Spurs rake each flank. There are ways
of owning something so hard, it drops.

Down Canyon

Coyotes howl,
corrupt night's
hush, raucous

as fraternity boys
whoop whoop
when you stumble,

trip, beer sloshing
wrist. Singled out—
yip-yip-yip—

the circle tightens
on fresh haunch.
Oaks turn away,

owl rips mouse.
College girl, dirt
in your mouth—

staring at clouds—
white cotton bra
flung into scrub.

The Birds

Filming in Bodega Bay, Alfred Hitchcock
dyed Tippi Hedren blonde, put her in a tight, lime skirt,
polished her nails pain red. His camera followed her girdled rump
through frame after frame. She wore pickax heels. And pearls.

Remember the movie?

After the town's attacked, crows wait like thugs
on Calvary. Tippi crosses their gaze, walks as if she has an egg
balanced between her thighs. Into a dead run, she slams
inside the glass phone booth.

Silence. Tippi puts the phone to her ear.

Flap. Shadow. Shadow. Swoop,
flap—cauldron—knife wings.
Black jabbing beaks. Claws.
He promised he'd use fake birds.

A real gull crashes through.
Scree Scree Scree
Cheeks, skin, mouth. Ripped raw as fish.

Sinking, blouse torn, her bloody hand
presses the glass.

Hitchcock calls for take after take.

Tippi gets back up. At the premiere, top billing
goes to the male star. I can never remember
who he was.

Queen

Look how her attendants tremble to serve! Groomed, fed
in an amber womb, she dreams not of them, but an April morning

she flew away, briefly free, from her room of wax. Too fast
the sky grew black with pursuers drunk on her musk. They burrowed

her body, spent their sex. She beat loose, rose once more. In the high silence
her eye compounded ovals, waterways, wildflowers—

space. Clarity. What tiny general ordered
her back? Enthroned, choked in gold, she spills forth eggs, two

thousand today, two thousand tomorrow. For five years. Seven. Workers bump
back and forth, their wings dusted with the forsaken world. They bear lotus,

lavender, attar of roses. Flightless, thick, she drowses in the hum.
Called back by dream, she lifts her head, crawls on trampled wing toward the other

realm she'd known. One part sky. One of brook. Bells of open-throated petals.

Guillotine, a Love Poem

You are my guillotine, crossbar and uprights of timber—
make tight the leather straps. I am but cargo in the donkey cart.
Deaf confessor, grant a penitent her last words:

For throwing myself at your feet, I deserve censure
most severe. A nod from you has sealed my fate in crimson
wax. Thus does desire doom love's aristocrat.

Hold my hair from my neck, adjust the lace at my throat.
Pray be gentle when you place my head in the lunette.
May my blood cement the happiness lovers know.

What's that? The crowd shouts for more than a thud
in the basket below? Executioner, make the oblique
blade sing. I leave open my eyes. *Be Quick!*

The Worst Gift

The worst Christmas. My dad two months dead,
I skulk through Poly High. Clustered girls fall silent as I pass.

Who bought our tree that year?

Below its tinsel, Mother lifts a package wrapped in green foil,
corners neat. Inside, a wicker box filled with buttons, Swiss
shears. Lift-out trays. A plastic container, her note taped
to its top: *Assorted Pins.* Like her stitch, the script is swift.
Intricate. I have a writer's hands. Take-out dinner hands.
My father's large knuckles.

Today, a seam rips. I retrieve the woven box, careful with its broken lid.
It holds my young mother shopping downtown. She selects thread.
Needles in graduated sizes, a red tomato pincushion. Everything
a daughter would need for mending.

Makeup

Mother tilts up her chin, blind eyes closed
as if receiving a benediction. I stroke foundation
across her brow, down the nose, blend liquid beige
into crevices bracketing her mouth. The last time I touched
her face, my hands were small—shy tourists
to glamour. The vanity drawer exhales clouds
of powder that rise, sift back to the bottom. Lacquered
strands of dark-dyed hair stick to its wood. Her arsenal of pots
and wands are used up. Colors outmoded. I dig a nail
into a dried-out crater of rouge. Pat dabs of pink on her cheeks.
Mother's skin sinks under my touch. Here's her lipstick—
Cherries in the Snow—worn flat to the rim. I swab
enough to redden her mouth. She rolls her lips
evening-out the color. Holding a mirror close to her face,
I say we're done. She turns her head this way
and that, seeing herself beautiful.

Little Scientists

On Sundays our mother dropped off my brothers
and me at the First Church of Christ Scientist,
drove off with a cigarette burning in the ash tray.

We sat straight in hard little chairs while God was spooned
into us like exotic salad—omnipotent, omnipresent—
that was better for you than it tasted. We wanted to be Methodists

like our friends. Wanted to be pals with cool Jesus in their Easter
coloring books. When they went to camp, we bent
to the Bible and Mrs. Burrell, who said pain

was all in our heads. Our bottoms froze. Mother ran late,
always, half the day lost. Confined to bed, Grandma read
the Sunday lesson from *Science & Health with Key to the Scriptures*,

fingers stiff as crickets clamped to the page. She refused
aspirin and spirits, convinced to the end that death
was just a misunderstanding.

Les Vieilles

(The old women)

Where are they going—the old bone women bent over a stick?
Their history humped on their backs. Who sees them?

Grandma languished in a high-rise
for the frail. I'd visit late, brush her cheek with wine-
soured lips. Old men clattered past on marionette wires. Flat
on her back, her bottom lip hung slack as an empty swing,
hands resting above the covers like misplaced mittens. I forked
cold potatoes into her mouth, eyes fastened on the clock.

Her fingers once tied coins in my hankie. She taught me
to make do, took night classes in upholstery. Needlework. Tiny stitches
for doll dresses in organdy and lace. In her kitchen we drank sweet
foam root beer. The Dodgers were killing 'em on the radio.
I'd fall asleep in the tufted arms of an armchair she'd redone, brass
tacks hammered tight as drums. In the institution's arctic quiet,
I wanted to hear her say I was still her *best girl*.

*

Paris. I stand in line at a chocolate shop near Place Vendôme.
Two ancient French beauties—stoic in battered fur—
wheel an older one to the front. Small as a nest egg after the War,
she points a trembling claw toward a truffle in a gold cup.
I buy darkest ganache. Mother's favorite. At every visit
I repeat my name. She regards me with good will. I could be anyone.
I place a chocolate between her lips. Mother sucks its molten heart.
Opens her mouth for more.

*

In my pocket is a ballet ticket to see Balanchine's *Jewels*. Ten years ago
the ballerina was thin as filament. Diamond hard.
Now she's 40, her last year on stage. Her line—an elegant stretch
of arm and leg—tricks the eye away from a waist grown thick.
She whips out 26 fouettés. Spins on one leg. Scissors
the other. The audience goes wild. On her toes all her life
so close to God—must she walk flat-footed into heaven?

*

In my family, the men die young. Leave their wives
to their daughters. We hand them off to live with strangers
chattering in Tagalog. Mother tucked her mother away.
I put mine in a house of sick women. In distant rooms, narrow
beds, they turned one-by-one to face the wall—*Little Grandma,
Aunt Mattie, Mother, Grandma Marie.*

*

At the Café Danton, two old ladies sit in low winter sun
savoring pots of tea, morsels of cake. When they laugh,
they hold their hands in front of their mouths. Putting on coats,
the friends kiss each other on both cheeks. One stumbles
over a boy's outstretched feet. Lips outlined in black, his girlfriend
pouts, examines strands of her hair. I want to pinch the girl hard.
Écoute! What you haven't lost yet will crack your heart.

In Produce

The woman pulls at her fuzzy gray hair, paces near a pile of heirloom
tomatoes muttering, *I'm too old to have a baby, baby, baby.*
Big, knobby necklace around her neck.
Talking in public like that. *I am Spirit. Baby's coming
any minute.* Mothers pull their children away.

Fingers splayed across her stomach, the woman coos
my baby my baby between stacks of glossy eggplant
and turnips raw as love against a brick wall.
She looks around, eyes overbright.

The assistant manager steers her toward the door.
Underbreath, a shopper says, *There goes one crazy old girl.*
But what if she has good news—carries just what we hunger
for—wouldn't you stop?
Wouldn't you make a place in the straw?

Songbird

If only I had my mother's light soprano, my brother's harmony. When I was cut from Glee Club, mother bought a piano. Hired a woman to make me *musical*.

Week after week, I ravaged the scales. Saying she could do no more, my teacher quit the day after my recital. I fell into the silence of books. Word's music.

Mother loved show tunes. Rodgers and Hammerstein. Emphysema's fist gripped her chest, she kept on singing. I'd follow her voice through dissonant

rooms of the Alzheimer's home. The last time I saw her, she sang to me, half in whisper, *'Bye 'Bye, Blackbird*. In perfect pitch.

Huntington Beach, November

My mother's hand is warm as a hamster in mine. Blind,
she sits next to me on a bench overlooking the Pacific. Gulls
describe the glint below. Barnacled pier. Bundling her, an old sweater hangs

past her fingers. Her floppy hat lifts. Dips. Still wearing glasses, huge lenses
smeared, her eyes are the color of scuffed shoes. At first, she begged to leave
the group home. Now, she makes no requests. Also no complaints. Mother eats.

Mother sleeps. Is washed and changed. Today they've put her in another patient's clothes—
pink fleece kittens. When I was little, I was terrified I would lose her at the market.

I want to pin her to my sleeve like milk money. The surf churns
the sand. Chocolate cone dropped to her lap, she turns the other way.

God,

Rock in my shoe, tight underpants,
cut that won't heal. Holder of
my balloon payment note.
Insomnia, no refills left
on my painkillers—
Oh Indistinct Divinity:
hand that tosses fire opals
on a broken sea, where are You?
Contrail, fleeting Merlin moon—
down on my knees, beseeching
the sky—I have never known
what You wanted. Still I dig,
nails filthy and cracked.
Show me.

On His Last Birthday

Dad strutted in flush, humming. Monogrammed cuffs. Dinner cold, so what?
We lit 42 candles for him.

Dead by October. Never saw his sons grow. Walked his daughter to the altar. Forever Jack
of Diamonds, high-cheeked. Buffed nails. Shuffle, deal—that's how I remember him.

Roll the dice again. Say he survives, gambles for matchsticks with palsied
hands. I clip his toes. Button his pants. Cover his debts. Anything for him.

The Wait

On the night of dark whales
  someone dies off
    the California coast.

A mortician goes to work, doesn't come
  home. Palms follow, sweep fallen
    stars into the sea.

His daughter counts foghorns like sheep.
  Some nights she begs the moon
    on her bed not to go.

/Antidote

Using a Number 2 pencil, circle
the word in each line that does not belong

Barbie	Dandelion	Airbus	Morgue
Thong	Shoe	Ocean	Wax
Column	Lamp	Sitcom	Taxes
Boot	Vow	Crusade	Jazz
Key	Masque	Harpoon	Gin
School	Military	Apron	Candle
Drought	Pistol	Cello	Brassiere
Grass	Shroud	Marble	Spark

Suite 286
Long Beach, CA 90803

Office: 562.598.7575
Toll Free: 855.305.7575
Cell: 562.773.7575
Fax: 480.998.2883
jack.dilday@ffec.com

N. Jack Dilday

DILDAY & ASSOCIATES
Investment Planning and Management

10/29/15

Dear Ron,

Here is the book of poems by
my sister I promised you a
few months ago. Please enjoy.

Jack

Dilday & Associates operates under First Financial Equity Corporation (FFEC). Member FINRA, SIPC. Securities and Investment advisory services offered through FFEC.
N. Jack Dilday's CA Insurance License #0A37029

Las Vegas

On his last spree, an ambulance brought our dad back after collapsing at the craps
table. Three days into a good run, tie flipped over one shoulder, cuffs rolled
up. He held his wrists out front like a faith healer,

the dice so hot they shook like saved souls.

The van drove away, Dad in the back. Fat tires rolled soft up the grade. A jackpot moon
spilled silver dollars over his face. The sun started to come up slow, shimmery
as footlights climbing a showgirl's thigh.

Wheeled into the ER at 5:45, Dad bet the nurse he'd be out before we left for school.

We woke to the whispers of short days. Words chipped from tight lips.
The adults walked into rooms, shut doors. My brothers and I grew quiet
with each other. Fifty years later, what's different is how clearly

I see my father doubling down. Other players dip into the rent. The college money
to stack their chips next to his. He stands a little ahead of himself, light and easy
on the balls of his feet—a man high on luck watching the wheel spin—

our father in the desert. He'd put the sun and moon on the table. Anything could happen.

Chance

Thinking a dime could hold off death,
my brother saved them in a white sock.
The first came from the floor
of a dead man's car. *Keep it kid*,
a cop said tossing him the coin.
My brother drove the body
to the morgue. He figured odds
were good the same dime
wouldn't be in two fatal
crashes. Thirty years later,
a doctor sees a slide of white
cells piling up like jackknifed
cars. Hospitalized, my brother
held the dime in his hand.
Our Dad and his rabbit foot
went the same way. Me?
I don't believe in luck.
Not really. Still I never pass
a lost dime without picking
it up, turning it over to see
Mercury's profile, his head
clad with silver wings.

Birds Caught in Windows

I come from a button jar filled with blue eyes

Father the undertaker
       selling flowers   and a funeral
       to a woman with a baby

        the flag   the casket

Red plaid shirts at Grand Canyon's rim
       matched set   loose stitched

His bullwhip bought as a joke
       stand there *snap snap*

Sprung from school   Dad & me at the track
       daily double   50 to 1

Ambulance at night
       his blood bag yellow eyes bruises
       whispering nurses *what? what?*

Secret hideouts
       fig tree attic back of the Buick

& charms
       gold dice tux studs nudie deck

Folding chairs strangers dry kisses
       flyaway hit walls flyway hit glass

Your Chair

for my father

You've died.
Risen on two
ghostly legs,
disappeared.
No longer do
you fill this
straight-backed
seat. Absence
beatifies. Yours
brings glory to
the lowly things
you owned. If you returned, the chair would not hold
you as you were. It goes on being dark oak. You go
on being gone.
Did you think
you gave it
purpose? Look—
it shines where
your thighs
sank gratefully
onto wood.
Don't worry.
Your chair
is still here.

Breaking Up With the Moon

nights I stumbled   barefoot from bed   to cold window

courtyard deserted   glass held my breath   I looked for   myself

times I fell under   your sweep   as spoils   brushed from a table

wine glossed   my lips   splintered waiting   naked   taken

apart at parties   taverns   in cars   my alabaster lover

gibbous other   face half cadaver   half shadow   swallowed

my youth   your swollen mouth   spilled fibs   silver distortions

keep your gin fizzes   black holes   nightly show

Family Curse

                                   Red flags. White caps. My brother casts
off in a twelve-foot outboard he starts with a jerk,

sputters into chop. Our grandfather waded through a flooded cellar

to fix a broken bulb. Uncle Leland flew. See his stunt plane loop-de-loop.
Stall. Dive nose down. Scorch, burn.

At our family's Fourth of July, Dad's brother Dick watches us play as he pours starter fluid
on cold briquettes, a hidden ember within. Fire snakes up, takes his arm, his torso.
His five year-old daughter's face.

If there's a common destiny, ours is to sail as ash on water.

Brother's boat has no compass. No radio. He points the bow toward Catalina, 26 miles
off coast. His cooler's full of frozen bait. In Avalon Bay, the mackerel are biting.

Wind whips off his cap. Hollows the horizon. Between the pitch of ten-foot rollers,
the island rises like a sub, sinks from sight. He fights for the rudder with both hands.

                                For five hours, Dad stands on the jetty. Sea knives
slice his face, salt-spotted shoes. Lighting cigarette on cigarette, he searches the froth
for his crazy kid.

Who knows what promises he makes to the sea?

To the red tip at the end of his hand? Out of the dark, the Coast Guard tows a boat,
his boy's pale face at the rail.

Falling in Love

More like drowning, descent
through murky light. Kelp ropes
your feet. Invisible hands
lift the dress over your head.
Your breasts sway. Are you
free? Brine and sting,
you flail toward the sky.
He grabs your hair,
dives. Deep down green,
his mouth finds yours.
Open your lips. Take
air in. It's him.

Nobody's Business But Ours

We're dressed for a cousin's wedding: In the back row, crepe-eyed Dad, mouth sloped
down, his hand solid on Mother's shoulder.

Mortuary school. Marriage. Straight into the family job, four kids.

Nights the county coroner called, Dad pushed back from dinner, drove off in a van.
A gurney and canvas sack were in the back. At disasters, he'd pick up what was left—
someone's glasses, a severed hand. Shoes.

After work, he soaked his arches in formaldehyde. I'd stare at his white feet, flat
as bottom fish. At Rotary, other men talked accounting, dentistry. Ours kept
work to himself—the stupid kids killed
drag racing, drunks he hauled from five buck
motels. Doll-sized coffins he sold to new mothers.

Nights he sat up drinking, he'd look in as he passed our rooms.

Some weeks he disappeared without saying where. He'd come back with a Kachina doll
for me. A trick lariat for the boys. For my mother, a squash blossom necklace.

Did he think trinkets could protect us? A man who kept death's ledger? At the end
of day, he'd come up our walk to the only house happy to see him.

Three Days in Portland

             Lost, I'm going wrong
on one-way streets—turn back, run a red light, miss
the drawbridge. Detoured, I keep passing the same strip
sign *Come See What You Get for a Buck Twenty-Five.*
I haven't bought a lot—nylon poncho

I've worn non-stop, mugs of Stumptown that hit my gut hard
as a late night knock. Jackhammers jerk me awake every morning.

             Something else is off—
everywhere—beards. Plaid. A teen mom stares out a café window, oily braid,
blue wing inked on her breast. Wedged in her arm, the newborn wet-sucks
a nipple big as a doorbell.

I wolf down a bowl of goat cheese and bacon macaroni. Hate this place more.

             Something's wrong—
stalled on a bridge driving to my brother buried at River View, the rented Dodge
shakes the way his pine box trembled over the void. They lowered him
there, the dirty Willamette drooling below.

             His stone shines
in soaked lawn as I slip toward him, rain strafing my ankles,
my face. I swear anything would be better than this
for the tawny boy I taught to swim.

Boy on the Subway

Beautiful boy lounging
on the train, your collar
pulled up, a girl curled

against your rib. I watch
you and think of a lover
who kept me one winter.

When the subway pulls in
you shrug off the girl, zip
your jacket to jaw. Saunter

through the heavy doors.
She's on your heels, hand
stretched toward the nape

of your neck. Callow son,
watch where you prowl.
If she is fatherless,

she'll follow you on the long
ride to the shore. You think
you've escaped. She waits

your next breath. Beautiful boy,
you are air. She, drowning.

.

The Coast Starlight

If I could see you again, when the train comes tonight I'd leave
this messy bed, climb on board, feel my way

down the corridor, rails running rockety rockety up my spine, ride
north through fields of strawberries, train undulating like a silver eel. Towns reel

out, scatter of houses, clumped shadows erase everything but my face/your face
in the glass. Hills give to a stretch of beach set with white linen, lit by the lace-

draped moon. The tide rips out its stitches and re-embroiders the hem. Gathering.
Unraveling, and you weaker each time—Long Beach Bainbridge Ellensburg   Portland.
.

Hotel Room

Walls. No more than my body fits
between bed and door. I kick
off shoes that pinch, the thick wool
hose. Stripped to a silk shift, I sit
at bed's edge watching a violet sky
pass into black. Tomorrow they'll bury
my brother. The night is young.
I could do up my hair, head
down to the bar—it's worked
for me before. The suitcase waits
like a dog at my feet. What if I skipped
town? Let the trees stand
for his eulogy. This room
of no memory knows nothing of me.
I'll wake early, change
into everyday flats, walk backward
to last week. Finding me gone,
the hotel maid will pass a quick cloth
through the bureau drawers,
close the door, my black felt hat under her coat.

Twelve Days Before the Fire

Summer has stayed too long,
holding the folds of her skirt
above the jaundiced tide.
Dazed crows perch on wires;
the widow eucalyptus waits
in gray rags. Roses drop, wan,
exhausted. I follow a jet's
crawl across the bland sky.
It's been 90 degrees forever.
October's gone. It doesn't matter.
I hoard my breath like water.

Root over Feather

At a pause, the pianist lifts his wrists, stares at his hands
       as if they don't belong to him, two strange birds poised
            mid-air. The strings come up—murmuring, lush—

as he turns back to the keyboard, weaves root over feather,
       a nest of spider silk. Next to me, your eyes are closed, body
           swaying in time with the clarinet.

Last night we stood facing each other across the bed. Silent

as an abandoned theatre, you held your hands to your sides.
       Mine were balled shut. Who composed our mute world?
       Did I, wood dove, tear out your throat?

What Doesn't Come Home

Tail erect, nose in the weeds, my deaf dog
ignores me. I stomp to where she digs. She looks

up holding a cat's disembodied head
in her mouth. Eyes wide, it died fierce, fangs

split into a hiss. What hunger
tempted it into the dark?

What shadow trailed after? I chop
my hand down, signaling the dog, *Drop It.*

We head home past posters of lost cats nailed
to telephone poles. Bleached flyers for Frankie,

Tumbler. Socks. The missing follow.
A frozen yowl. The hunter's hot mouth.

Dominion

over all the earth and over every living thing   Genesis 1:26

My husband and the neighbor stand divided
by an invisible property line. The neighbor says
our new fence should be set ten feet back.
City shoes sliding over loose rock, my husband
paces off the stakes, surveyor's map in hand, argues
he's already sacrificed five feet. Neither man
has ever dug a hole, sunk concrete, stretched a wire.

This is the first real property they've ever owned, earned
hard inch by inch, from year to neck-tied year. The men glare,
cross their arms, each one guarding his acre
of oak, cactus. Boulders iced with lichen.

Slow Morning

I zip a parka over my robe to feed the dogs. Cold, still midnight
in their metal bowls. Home from world tour, the frog choir sings the old songs,
but in German. Puppy wanders in from scouting the yard—her nose
can barely contain the news.

White clouds, blue sky. Some days it's the other way around.

Sun-startled, I squint. See a cricket wave a scepter
at the bees. The azaleas. What other tricks
does the world have up its sleeve?

The poinsettias hang on all year. Adamant as false teeth.

Channeling Colette, I write in bed. Add doves, brash
coffee, a vanishing train.

Every generation ends up as ghosts. I sense
them drift into theatres, take seats
between customers. You never know whose hand
reaches for your popcorn. Peter Lorre's were small as a girl's.

I crawl back in bed. Sheets funky as clothes in a consignment
shop. Hit and run, no witnesses. My mother hoarded a green velour
ladies Stetson. Her mother bought it for her with money
from the coffee tin. Mother's affection for the hat
outlasted her memory of me.

The Other Side of the Bed

Listen, you can grow to hate a man
sleeping on his back. Boat-bottom
throat sucking light, dark,

even the webs from the room.
You stare up at cornered spiders
holding on with sticky pluck.

You can grow to hate the way his head
dents the pillow like his mama's lap,
mouth open. Greedy baby.

Sleep-gorged, he grips the sheet
as if it's his binky, grunts every time
you tug your scrap of it back.

Watching his gullet bubble and flutter,
a flounder—but louder—you might consider
fitting your pillow over that face.

You could grow used to sleeping alone,
dainty you, quiet under your ruffled cover.
You'll get a cat, a silk quilt. A pink kimono.

What We Can't Give Up

He sleeps face-up, arm flung—
I watch, wide awake all night. High

fire season. The danger arrow
at the county firehouse stuck on *Extreme*.

Humidity low, we stay close to home.
The last evacuation he hauled boxes. I grabbed

our dog's ashes. For five nights firefighters
from as far away as Idaho trudged back from the line,

their heads hot, swollen. Hills exploded. Our ridge curdled
in serpents of smoke. My husband worried for the dove

sitting two eggs in the tree outside our door. If they came
would rescuers crash through? Trample the nest?

I called forth the sky, commanded blue to pour
through every window, fling its watery body across

our marriage bed. Spare the dove her nest.

After Your Diagnosis

I imagine how it must be now—you swallow your chemo,
head against a sofa back, TV turned low. Your silver cat plays

with pillow fringe, shapes pass in and out like moths. Your wife
carries in groceries. Youngest daughter won't leave her room.

You and I grew up in a house like this—Dad home from the hospital
for awhile. We know how it goes. When we talk on the phone

it's of books and cars, a pact weighs our words. For every loss,
someone is set adrift. I'll come after, put one hand on your wife's shoulder,

unfold your daughter's fist with the other. On your birthday, you told me
your first job was sweeping mums from a florist's floor. You were ten.

One day, I'll tell them that.

Market Day, Rue de Buci

Big American guy—my husband—among the French. Standing in line,
he swipes sweat from his brow, hot and caulked with salt.
He takes out his wallet, pays for soda, plums. The girl
behind him pulls her basket up, festive with foie gras,
three kinds of cheese. A glistening chicken with feathered
feet. She wears her hair in a high ponytail, cropped bangs
the color of burled wood. He helps hold her basket
as she searches for change, lips plump as cherries
in a bone china bowl. Walking back to me,
he turns once to look at her. I'd like to tell her
thank you, angel of desire. Right on the street
he kisses me so long my mind flies
to that poster taken on VE Day.
The sailor and his girl.

Going Nowhere

Feet blistered and glued to our shoes, we stump through the Louvre—
Mona LisaVenus Diana—stop, silenced before Michelangelo's slaves. Limping

back to the hotel, we are middle-aged. Married. The night we met, this man ripped
off my dress. I squeeze after him into the stuttering elevator. Up we go, two

pieces of toast. The cage stalls short of the sixth floor, filigreed gate opening,
slamming shut. A vertical coffin made for one. My husband punches

the buttons, refuses to join my old song—*The cable will snap! We'll crash!*

He tries the red knob. A woman's voice floats in. She will save us, *bien sûr*, but only
in French, which I happen to speak. We must wait, *s'il vous plaît*, one hour. The lift slips,

shudders. Belly to belly, lunch bubbles between us—bread, cream sauce, cheese. My husband
shifts from leg to leg, whistling tunelessly his nervous tic. For the first time in 25 years,

I can't turn away. Can't storm out. Our cage darkens. In Paris two honeymooners kiss
on a bridge, the setting sun blushes rose, blushes gold. Stuck

between floors, my husband and I breathe in, breathe out. Something nudges
my thigh. I check my watch. "Fifteen more minutes," I say. "Time enough."

Zen Metro

Anonymous bodies push me past bellies,
elbows. Winter coats. I stumble
into a circle of six Buddhist monks
in sandals and robes.
Shaved heads, yellow plum smiles,
they stand with one hand
on the center pole,
the other on a brother monk's shoulder.
When the train cuts and bucks,
everyone struggles but them.
A man bellows, phone at his ear.
Squeal of brake, steel
against steel. Tumbling swarm.
The monks sway, dandelions
in a summer meadow.
Up front, station lights beckon
the train out of the dark.
Gathering folds of cloth, the brothers
glide away in silent congress. *Follow.*
Become singing bowl.
Become lotus flower.

Indiscretion on Rue Royale

Framed in the tea room's stippled mirror,
the couple can't see me watching her
pour hot chocolate for him, ladling
stiff curls of whipped cream from
a silver bowl. Pastries shaped
like Russian domes sit untouched
between them. Her breath ripples
across the pelts of pale fur slipping
from her bosom as the man leans in.
Longish hair, black shirt, he examines
her hands as if they were artifacts, presses
his lips deep into her palms. Kisses the right
one. Kisses the left. Eyes on her face, he holds
her hands to his mouth like sipping cups.
Tiny lines crisscross her face the way
a cracked Botticelli begs fresh oils. Dusk
ushers blue into the room. Bill paid,
the man helps the woman rise, rearranges
the great mink on her shoulders. They pass
by me. I stare at my lap, palms throbbing.

On the Canal Saint Martin

The man with the thin tie says, "Pardon,"
takes a seat on my bench. In silence,
we share the water waltzing with the sky,
the sleepy-eyed apartment buildings
waking up. A matron picks across cobblestones,
bare ankles laced into espadrilles, trailing lavender
soap and her morning cigarette. Bobbing at the bank
is a barge fresh-painted with red lacquer trim.
White shirts swing from its stern, ready to fly.
The tourist bateau swishes by; people wave
from the deck, their voices lost on a lick of foam.
A taxi blasts three times. Just like that, *crack*,
the day splits in two.

Beautiful

Of course, of course, Paris is beautiful,
as a bat is beautiful, dark wings
backlit. In the underground Metro
a broken-backed man waits
for a train, more crab
than fellow creature. Place Pigalle's
parade of grotesques shoves by—
hags, drunks in oily clothes.
Pretty boys cinched at the waist jut
their hips, faces like hearts, tense.
The bent-over man sees nothing
but shoes, phlegm. Petrified gum.
He scuttles from side to side
the way a dog dodges
the boot. Beautiful Paris. The bat
must have its crippled spider.

Deadlines, Musée d'Art Moderne

Near closing, I hurry through
an exhibition by artists who knew
they were dying. A wall
of seascapes, the painter adrift
in a lifeboat, head back, face
gashed in acid yellows. Next gallery,
sick infants whimper from speakers
hidden in an empty hospital bed.
Their soft little sobs follow me
through the rooms. On a video monitor,
I watch the filmmaker punch the air,
scream at the camera. He paces,
curls his long body under a desk.
His eyes bore into mine: *This
is terror. Remember it.*

Five o'clock. The guard escorts me
into winter dark. I walk along stone facades,
chambers brightening behind drapes,
thinking of my notebooks, words
lifeless as specimens glued to paper.
In the rented apartment, my husband naps,
his big, green coat tossed over a chair.
Love, paint us into a Chagall sky,
surround me with birds and blue
horses. Take hold of my hair.

Anorexia Mirabilis

A damselfly,
wings transparent as a blue bottle, feels
its way across my window.
            Animate blade, barely
visible as when I dwindled unnoticed
after losing a man who wanted
a woman more slender.
            Cast aside, I lose myself
to the *miracle maids* of the Middle Ages.
In the plump rooms of Vienna, I refuse
food. With lush ardor,
            I renunciate
the body's awfulness, slowly become
glowing bone. Devotion is not without
its tender fanatics.
            To master desire,
Saint Catherine took one teaspoon of herbs
each day. I live on lettuce until faint headed.
            Arriving to fatten me, Mother locks
my door, forces sacher torte into my mouth. I choke.
Kirsch burns my throat.
            The insect freezes. I tap
the window, trace its head, linger
over the glassy wings.

Flight

Above the coastal plain, low clouds thin to Spanish lace. Undo
        your shoulder blades, become the sleek wings
                of a mourning dove. Roll the bone bundles loose

in their sockets. Where spine pinches nerve, gravity's straight pins bind.
        Slip free. In this world, you have traveled as a stranger in heavy
                shoes. Unlace the leather, lift one bare foot. Then the other.

Notes

"Your Chair" is after Gerhard Richter's *Stuhl im Profil*, oil on canvas.

"Hotel Room" is after Edward Hopper's *Hotel Room*, 1931, oil on canvas.

"The Coast Starlight" is in memory of my brother Randy Dilday.

"After Your Diagnosis" is for my brother Jack Dilday.

Acknowledgments

My sincere thanks to the editors of the journals in which these poems first appeared, a few in earlier forms or under different titles.

Atlanta Review: "Nobody's Business But Ours"
Cairn: "Market Day, Rue de Buci"
California Quarterly: "Twelve Days Before the Fire"
CALYX: "Childless" and "Songbird"
Caveat Lector: "Breaking Up with the Moon" and "Slow Morning"
Compass Rose: "Little Scientists" and "Mortician's Daughter"
Existere—Journal of Arts and Literature (Canada): "Down Canyon"
Folio: "*Deadlines*, Musée d'Art Moderne"
Griffin: "Pony Ride"
Jabberwock Review: "Anorexia Mirabilis" and "I Want"
Limestone: "Going Nowhere"
Natural Bridge: "Three Days in Portland"
New Ohio Review: "Dear Doris Day"
Nimrod International Journal: "Elegy for Dead Words" and "The Wallow Variations"
Painted Bride Quarterly: "/Antidote"
Pearl: "On the Canal Saint Martin"
Pembroke Magazine: "The Worst Gift"
Permafrost: "After Your Diagnosis" and "The Female Line"
Poem: "Hand to Hand"
Prairie Schooner: "Makeup" and "The Wait"
Quiddity International Literary Journal: "Les Vieilles" and "Zen Metro"

Red Cedar Review: "Blind Date with Baudelaire"
The Same: "Beautiful," "Guillotine, a Love Poem" and "Indiscretion on Rue Royale"
Sanskrit: "Family Curse"
South Carolina Review: "The Other Side of the Bed"
Southern Humanities Review: "In Produce"
Southern Poetry Review: "Dominion"
Stand (UK): "Big Boy" and "God,"
Sou'Wester: "Queen"
Storyscape Journal: "Birds Caught in Windows," "Build to Suit," "Hotel Room" and "Your Chair"
Valparaiso Poetry Review: "Flight"
WomenArts Quarterly Journal: "Parties" and "What We Can't Give Up"
Zone 3: "Las Vegas" and "Root over Feather"

I respectfully thank Gregory Orr for selecting my first book for the ABZ Poetry Prize. Thank you John McKernan and ABZ Press for publishing *Lunette*.

To Laure-Anne Bosselaar, poet and friend, thank you for wise counsel bringing the book to its final form. Thanks also to Holly Prado for suggestions made to the book in its infancy.

To my poetry family, thanks for close reading and insight: Christine Kravetz, Amy Michaelson, and Susan Chiavelli, with particular thanks to Perie Longo for nurturing craft. For encouragement, special thanks to my extended writing circle: Sandy Giedeman, Lynn McGee, Robert Vaughan, and Elizabeth Call Enger.

To the poets who have guided my life in poetry, I thank Ellen Bass, Dorianne Laux, Joseph Millar and fellow workshop writers for their collective wisdom, generosity, and engagement. Thank you Mark Doty and Nick Flynn for extending my reach.

I was blessed with the best of brothers—Jack, Steve, and Randy Dilday. Warm gratitude to my chosen sister, Diane René, for lifelong friendship.

This book is for my husband, Chris Davis, whose love, optimism and belief in my work continue to sustain me.

About the Author

Pamela Davis, a third-generation Californian, received her BA in English from California State University at San Francisco. Before a career specializing in medical writing and editing, her work has taken her from a job in the family mortuary to living in Paris as a nanny, social work with mothers and children, administrator for a non-profit organization, and freelance journalism. She is a co-founder of the Independent Writers of Southern California. Her poems have appeared widely in journals including *Prairie Schooner, Existere—a Journal of Literature and Art (Canada), Southern Poetry Review, Valparaiso Poetry Review, Nimrod International Journal, Painted Bride Quarterly, Southern Humanities Review, Sou'Wester, Stand (UK), New Ohio Review, Caveat Lector*, and *Zone 3*. She received *Atlanta Review's* International Poetry Publication Award, and her work is included in the *Meridian Anthology of Contemporary Poetry*. She lives in the hills of Santa Barbara with her husband and two yellow retrievers.

CPSIA information can be obtained
at www.ICGtesting.com
Printed in the USA
FSOW03n1618040515
6904FS